Mary
Mother of Jesus

BARBARA HINTZE • ILLUSTRATED BY **JAMES PADGETT**

BROADMAN PRESS
Nashville, Tennessee

4242-32
ISBN: 0-8054-4232-4

Dewey Decimal Classification: J225.92
Subject heading: MARY, VIRGIN
Printed in the United States of America

Contents

A Song of Worship

Mary grew up in a Jewish home. The Bible does not tell us about her life when she was a girl. But, because we do know about the customs and the life of the people at that time, we can imagine what a day in Mary's life might have been like.

Early in the morning, Jewish women walked to the village well to get water. Let's imagine that Mary stood by the door of her home, waiting for her mother to walk with her to the well. As Mary waited, she watched the boys on their way to synagogue school.

As Mary and her mother walked to the well, they were joined by other women from the village. Mary carried a small pot for water, while her mother carried a large one.

Mary loved to walk to the well. She loved to listen to the women talk and to play with other children who came to the well. Mary could smell the flowers, and she could see mountains nearby. Perhaps she whispered a prayer: "Thank you, God. Thank you for such a beautiful place to live."

When Mary and her mother returned from the well, they made bread. Mary's mother got out the barley and sat down at the grinding stone. Mary helped her turn the stone, and soon they had enough meal. Then Mary poured water into a bowl, and her mother added a small piece

of the yeast she had saved from the day before. Together, Mary and her mother added the meal to the liquid, making dough. They mixed and mashed the dough with their hands until it was just right. Then they left the dough to rise.

There were other tasks to be done, and we can be sure that Mary helped her mother do them all. Mending had to be done, the house had to be cleaned, the meals had to be cooked. On some days, the clothes had to be taken to the stream to be washed. Perhaps there was a goat to be milked.

Sometimes Mary's mother worked to weave cloth for their clothes. Mary was learning to weave. Sometimes she made mistakes. Then her mother helped her take out the mistake and do it right. Mary's mother wanted Mary to do her best.

So the day passed in happy, busy work. After the evening meal, Mary's family would gather for worship. Mary's father may have asked Mary to sing a psalm of thanksgiving. She might have sung something like this:

"The earth belongs to God.
Everything in all the world is his.
Praise the Lord, all his angels.
Praise his glory and his strength.
I will praise the Lord."

Thinkback: Make a list of some things that Mary probably liked to do.

How did Mary help her mother?

What song of worship did Mary sing? What song of worship do you like to sing?

A Song of Praise

As Mary grew up, she had many things to think about. We can be certain that she often talked to God.

Surely Mary thought often about the coming of the Messiah. For many hundreds of years, the Jewish people had been waiting for a Savior, a King, who would make them free. Many times Mary would have heard different teachers say, "The Messiah will surely come soon." Perhaps Mary wondered if she would ever see the Messiah. It would have been natural for Mary to pray often for God to send the Messiah soon.

Mary loved God with all her heart. As she grew older, we can imagine that she prayed: "Oh, God, now that I am a woman, let me be a good woman. Let me live as you would have me live."

One important thing Mary had to think about was her engagement to Joseph. The engagement likely became known in this way: One day, during a sabbath service, after the sermon and the reading of the scroll, the priest read Joseph's name and Mary's name together and told the congregation that they were to be married. Perhaps Mary prayed: "Thank you, God. Thank you for Joseph. Help me be a good wife to him."

Then, one day, Mary had a new, wonderful thing to think about. An angel appeared to her.

"Don't be afraid, Mary," the angel said. "God is with you. God will bless you in a wonderful way. You are to be the mother of a baby."

"But how can I have a baby?" Mary said to the angel. "I do not have a husband."

"Your baby will be the Son of God," said the angel. "You will name him Jesus. He will be the Savior, the King, the Messiah that all Israel has been waiting for."

The angel told Mary something else: "Your cousin, Elizabeth, who thought she was too old to have a baby, will have a son."

Then Mary told the angel, "I will serve God in any way he wants." And the angel went away.

Mary thought and thought about what the angel had said. She tried to understand. She had been chosen. She was to be the mother of the Messiah. Mary's heart was full of wonder and love.

Mary wanted to share her news with someone who would understand. So she went to Judea to visit Elizabeth who was her cousin.

Elizabeth was very glad to see Mary. "God has truly blessed you, Mary," said Elizabeth. "You will be the mother of the Messiah."

Mary's happiness was so great that she began to sing a new song:

"How I praise the Lord.
How I rejoice in God, who saves me.
For God, the mighty Holy One,
Has done great things for me.
He has not forgotten his promise.
The Messiah is coming soon."

Thinkback: Before the angel appeared to Mary, she had three things to think about. What were they?

What was the angel's message to Mary?

Read Mary's praise song again. What is your favorite praise song?

A Lullaby

Mary was very tired. She and Joseph had been traveling for days, all the way from Nazareth to Bethlehem. Mary had had a donkey to ride, but she was still very tired. Joseph was tired, too. He had walked all the way. But they were almost in Bethlehem, and when they got there, they could rest.

Mary thought back to the reason for their trip. The Roman government had decided to count the Jewish people. Every man must go back to the city which had been his family's home to be counted. Joseph's family was from Bethlehem, so Mary and Joseph had to go to Bethlehem.

The closer they got to Bethlehem, the more crowded the road was. Everybody, it seemed, was going to Bethlehem. Jewish people from all over the land were from Bethlehem and had to come back to be counted.

"I didn't know that this many people's families were from Bethlehem," Mary said.

Joseph was worried. "There won't be a place to stay left in the city," he said.

"It is almost time for the baby to be born, Mary. You need shelter. You need help," Joseph added.

"God will take care of us, Joseph," said Mary. "He will provide a place for us to stay. God will show us where the promised baby is to be born."

It was getting dark by the time Mary and Joseph got to Bethlehem. And, just as Joseph had said, there was no place to stay. Finally, they got permission to stay in a stable. It was clean and warm, and Mary was glad to be at the end of the journey.

The promised baby was born that night. Mary and Joseph thanked God for the baby. Then Joseph kept watch while Mary and the baby slept.

Sometime later, Mary was awakened by the sound of voices at the door of the stable. Joseph was talking to some shepherds.

"An angel told us to come here," the shepherds said. "The angel said we would find a baby in a manger. He said the baby was the Savior, the Messiah, the Lord."

Mary remembered all of the things that had happened to her. She thought about Jesus' birth there in the stable and the shepherd's visit. She remembered all of these things and thought about them often.

The shepherds looked at the baby and worshiped him. As they went away, they told everyone what had happened.

When Jesus was forty days old, Mary and Joseph took him to the Temple in Jerusalem. While they were there, a prophet named Simeon saw them. Simeon had been looking for the Messiah for a long time. When Mary and Joseph came in with Baby Jesus, Simeon knew this was the Messiah, the Savior. Simeon took Jesus in his arms and sang a song to him.

Perhaps Mary remembered some of Simeon's song and sang it to Jesus as a lullaby. Here is what Mary might have sung:

"Sleep, Baby Jesus.
You are the light that will shine on the nations.
You are the glory of God's people Israel.
You will be the greatest joy of many hearts.
Sleep, Baby Jesus."

Thinkback: Why did Joseph and Mary go to Bethlehem?

How do you think the shepherds felt when they saw the baby Jesus in the manger?

How do you think Simeon knew Jesus was God's Son, the Savior?

A Song About the Temple

"Joseph, are you sure we have everything? Jesus, did you remember to pack the sleeping mats? Is the donkey ready?" Mary was busy. She was trying to get everything and everyone ready for the trip. Many Hebrew people went to Jerusalem every year, to celebrate the Passover. And, now, Jesus was twelve years old. He was old enough to go along on the trip. Jesus was going with Mary and Joseph to Jerusalem, to the Temple there.

The trip from Nazareth to Jerusalem was almost like a big family picnic. The women visited and chatted. The men talked about the weather and the government. The children ran back and forth, shouting, laughing, and playing.

As the people got near the end of their journey, they were excited about seeing Jerusalem and the Temple. "The Temple is white and gold," Joseph may have told Jesus. "It is very large. You will be able to see it clearly."

Finally Mary and Joseph and Jesus caught sight of the city of Jerusalem. There were many big, wonderful buildings. And there, easier to see than anything else, was the Temple, the house of the Lord.

Perhaps Mary began to sing a song about the Temple and others sang with her. Here is a song they might have sung.

"I was glad when they said unto me,
'Let us go into the house of the Lord.'
Now we can see the Temple.
Now we can see the house of the Lord.
May there always be peace in Jerusalem.
May all who love the Lord be blessed."

Mary and Joseph and Jesus spent a week in Jerusalem, celebrating the Passover. This was a very special celebration for the Jewish people. They remembered how God had brought their forefathers out of the land of Egypt. They remembered how the angel of death had touched the firstborn son in every Egyptian home and made him die. But the angel of death had passed over the homes of the Jewish people. That is why the celebration is called the Passover.

When the feast was over, Mary and Joseph and others from Nazareth started home. Mary and Joseph did not know that Jesus had stayed behind. They thought he was with some of the others in the crowd.

But as the people began to make camp for the night, Mary and Joseph started looking for Jesus. When they could not find him, Mary became really worried.

"Where do you suppose he is?" Mary asked Joseph. "I was certain he was with one of our friends. But no one has seen him."

"We shall have to go back to Jerusalem to search for him," replied Joseph. "I do not know where he could be."

Mary and Joseph hurried back to Jerusalem. They looked for Jesus in a lot of places. They looked in the marketplace. They looked in the inn where they had stayed. But they could not find Jesus.

Finally, they went to the Temple. There he was, talking to the teachers of the Law.

"Where were you?" said Mary. "We have been so worried because we could not find you."

"Mother, you should have known where I was," answered Jesus. "You should have known that I would be here at the Temple, in my Father's house, doing my Father's business."

Thinkback: Why did Mary and Joseph and Jesus go to Jerusalem? What special meaning did the Passover celebration have for the Jewish people?

When Jesus was lost, where did Mary and Joseph find him? What was he doing?

A Sad Song

Many years passed. Mary watched Jesus grow to be a man. Jesus had learned many things from Mary and Joseph. Joseph taught Jesus to be a good carpenter. Mary taught him to always do his best.

Now, Jesus began to go from place to place, preaching and teaching and healing people. Mary stayed at home in Nazareth, but she often heard news of Jesus.

Mary heard about the crowds that followed Jesus. She heard about the special followers that he chose: Matthew and Peter and John and the rest.

Mary heard about some of the wonderful things that Jesus said. "I am the Way, the Truth, and the Life." "Be kind and loving to everyone, even your enemies." "Come unto me, all of you that are tired, and I will give you rest."

Mary also heard about the wonderful things that Jesus did. Mary heard how Jesus made blind people see. She heard how he made lepers well and how he made lame people walk. Mary heard that Jesus even brought dead people back to life.

For about three years, Jesus went about his business of preaching and teaching and healing. All this time, Mary kept loving him and thinking about him and praying for him, like mothers do when their children are away.

One day, Mary heard some bad news. "Jesus is in trouble," she heard people say. "The rulers of the Temple are looking for him. When they find him, they are going to put him in prison. They may even try to get him crucified."

"But, why?" Mary wondered. "Jesus has never done anything wrong. He has helped people all his life. Why would anyone want to hurt him?"

Many people believed Jesus to be the Messiah. The rulers of the Temple were jealous and afraid. They thought that the people would quit going to the Temple. The rulers thought that people would listen to Jesus, not to them.

"I must go to Jerusalem," Mary decided. "I must see Jesus. Maybe I can get him to come home to Nazareth with me. Jesus will be safe here."

But when Mary got to Jerusalem, it was too late. Jesus had been captured and tried. He had been sentenced to die, to be crucified.

Mary could not believe it. With some friends, she went to the place where the crucifixion was. Mary and her friends saw the crosses. And on the cross in the center, Jesus was placed. Mary watched as the soldiers mocked him.

Mary could not understand. Jesus was God's Son. Jesus was the Messiah. He had done nothing wrong. Why did he have to die? Mary was very sad. She may have remembered a sad song from the Scriptures:

"Is it nothing to you, all you who pass
by?

Look and see if there is any sorrow like
my sorrow."

Mary may have felt like adding her sad song to this one.

"I weep. Tears flow down my cheeks.
My strength is gone.
My son is gone.
The Messiah is gone.
The children of God have no future."

Thinkback: Why was Mary sad?

Why did the Temple rulers want to kill Jesus? Think of one thing Mary did when she was sad.

A Christian Song

Mary was sitting with others in a big room, waiting. Soon it would be time for the service to begin. As she waited, Mary thought back over the last few years. So much had happened!

Mary remembered the day Jesus was crucified. How sad she had been. She could not understand why Jesus had to die. All of Jesus' friends had been sad, too.

Then Mary remembered the wonderful morning, just three days later, when Jesus had risen from the grave. Mary remembered how hard it had been to believe that Jesus was really alive. But she had seen him. And Mary knew for sure that it was her son, that it was Jesus, come back to life.

Many others had seen Jesus after he had risen. They had come to understand that Jesus was the Messiah, the Savior, not only for the Jews, but for the whole world.

Mary remembered the day that Jesus went back to heaven. She had been standing with a large group of Jesus' followers, listening to Jesus talk. Suddenly the people had seen Jesus being carried up into the sky. Then, they saw two men in white robes standing nearby. "Jesus will come back again," they said. "Just like he went away, he will come again."

Gradually, others came to understand about Jesus and to believe in what he had done. Mary remembered how many of the believers had gone to other cities and started groups who would worship and believe in Jesus.

Now there was a group of Jesus' followers in Nazareth who met every Sunday to worship. Mary looked around. The room was full. The leader stood, and together the people sang a song about Jesus. Mary sang it, too. This is the song they sang:

"Great is the mystery of God.
Jesus Christ came to earth as a man.
Jesus lived a perfect life.
The angels served Jesus.
People all over the world believed in
Jesus.
Jesus was taken up to his glory in
heaven.
Praise the name of Jesus."

Thinkback: Think about the song that the followers of Jesus sang. How did Mary know that each part of the song was true?

What is your favorite song about Jesus? Could you make up a song about Jesus? Try it.

Reflections

Mary sang many songs in her lifetime. You have read about some of them in this book. What were some of the songs Mary sang?

There are many songs in the Bible. The songs that Mary sang are like some of the songs in the Bible. Look at the following passages in your Bible, and try to find the song of Mary that reminds you of the passage.

Psalm 24 Psalm 122
Luke 1:46-55 Lamentations 1:12
Luke 2:29-35 1 Timothy 3:16

What is your favorite Bible verse or passage? You could make a song using your favorite Bible passage. Why not try it?

SOME NEW TESTAMENT PLACES